Saints' Day Recipes

Celebrate Saints' Day with Mouth-Watering Recipes

BY

Stephanie Sharp

Copyright © 2020 by Stephanie Sharp

License Notes

Copyright 2020 by Stephanie Sharp All rights reserved.

No part of this Book may be transmitted or reproduced into any format for any means without the proper permission of the Author. This includes electronic or mechanical methods, photocopying or printing.

The Reader assumes all risk when following any of the guidelines or ideas written as they are purely suggestion and for informational purposes. The Author has taken every precaution to ensure accuracy of the work but bears no responsibility if damages occur due to a misinterpretation of suggestions.

Table of Contents

Introduction 6

   Saints' Day Almond Cookies 8

   Saints' Day Puto 10

   Camote Delight 12

   Bikoor Rice Cake with Caramel 14

   Halo Halo 16

   Arroz Valenciana 18

   Cassava Cake 21

   Pichi Pichi 24

   Coconut Jaggery Soul Cookies 26

   Lemon Chicken 29

   Nun Puffs 31

   Polish Doughnuts – Pączki 33

   Angel Food Cake 35

   Sugar Cookie Bars 37

Cinnamon spiced Soul cakes 40

DOUGHNUTS 43

Frosty Pumpkin Dessert 45

Tinga 47

Hot Cross Buns 49

Beef Stew 52

Grasshopper Pie 55

St. Martin's Mini Mice Cupcakes 57

Hungarian Cinnamon Bread 59

Rolled Spiced Rye Sticks 62

Apricot Currants Soul Cookies 65

Pecan Sweet Potato Balls 67

Shrimp Cheese Noodle Salad 69

Mashed Potatoes 72

Blueberry Pancakes 74

Chia Seed Spelt Bread 76

Conclusion 78

About the Author 79

Author's Afterthoughts 80

Introduction

Saints' Day is special for both Catholics and Protestants. In the western churches, they celebrate it on 1st November. In the eastern churches, they celebrate it on the first Sunday of Pentecost. The Roman Catholics deem it as a holy day, and they oblige thereby. The idea behind Saints' Day is to gather together and pray for the saints who have passed away. Ones can pray for the saints they have been following for years. They pray for them so they can enter heaven.

Some people visit their tombstones too. After their prayers, they indulge in a feast, and the feast usually connects them with the saints they follow.

In this book, you will find different types of recipes that will connect you with a different characteristic of a particular saint. You need to browse through the recipes and see which one would be best suited to honor the saints you followed.

All the 30 recipes are easy and delicious and somehow will connect you to the vibe of Saints' Day!

Saints' Day Almond Cookies

These soft and white almond cookies are perfect for celebrating Saints' day. It brings forth comfort to the eyes, too, when you look at the whiteness of the cookies.

Preparation Time: 15 minutes

Cooking Time: 10 minutes

Serves: 12

Ingredients:

- 1 cup (4 oz) almond flour
- 1 cup sugar
- 1 egg
- 1 tsp almond extract
- 2 1/2 oz ground almonds
- 1 pinch salt
- 3/4 tsp baking powder

Instructions:

Preheat your oven to 325 degrees F.

Add parchment paper on your baking sheet.

Beat the sugar, egg and almond extract in a bowl.

Add the dry ingredients and fold into dough. Knead well and let them refrigerate for 10 minutes.

Roll them out into 2 inch thickness and cut into long oval shape.

Add to the baking sheet. Then, bake for 10 minutes.

Serve with powdered sugar on top if needed.

Saints' Day Puto

This special puto not only tastes good but also looks heavenly. It is too adorable to look at.

Preparation Time: 15 minutes

Cooking Time: 25 minutes

Serves: 20

Ingredients:

- 2 eggs, beaten
- 1 tbsp baking powder
- 1 cup water
- 2 cups all-purpose flour
- 1/2 cup coconut milk
- 100 grams white sugar
- Banana leaves

Instructions:

Shift the dry ingredients in a bowl.

Cut the banana leaves into small rounds and add to your cupcake mould.

Beat the eggs with milk for 2 minutes. Add the water and beat well.

Add the dry ingredients and mix until it becomes smooth.

Add to the cupcake mould. Add to the steamer and steam for 20 minutes. Serve in room temperature.

Camote Delight

This is a healthy dessert recipe made using sweet potatoes. The butter adds softness and richness to it.

Preparation Time: 2 hours

Cooking Time: 20 minutes

Serves: 8

Ingredients:

- 2 cups sweet potato, boiled
- 1/2 cup sugar
- 1/2 cup butter
- 1 tsp vanilla extract
- 1/4 cup condensed milk
- 1 pinch salt

Instructions:

Mash the sweet potatoes finely in a large mixing bowl.

Add the butter and beat well.

Add the milk and sugar and beat again until everything combined.

Add muffin liners into your muffin mould.

Add the mixture into the liners generously. Refrigerate for 1 hour.

Add cubes of butter on top before serving.

Bikoor Rice Cake with Caramel

This dessert takes rice cakes to a whole another level. The caramel topping on top adds a layer of salty sweetness that melts in your mouth.

Preparation Time: 15 minutes

Cooking Time: 45 minutes

Serves: 8

Ingredients:

- 2 cups sticky rice
- 1 cup brown sugar
- 3 1/2 cups coconut milk
- 1/8 lb. butter

Topping:

- 3/4 cups coconut milk
- 3 tbsp flour
- 1 can (15 oz) condensed milk

Instructions:

Add the coconut milk with sticky rice in a saucepan.

Cook on medium low heat until the rice becomes tender.

Add the butter and sugar and mix well.

Grease a square pan and add the mixture.

For the topping, combine the coconut milk, flour and condense milk in a saucepan.

Cook for 15 minutes and stir continuously.

Add the topping onto the rice cakes. Serve warm.

Halo Halo

This dessert looks very fancy and tastes great too. You can use more fruit of your choice if you like.

Preparation Time: 10 minutes

Cooking Time: 40 minutes

Serves: 8

Ingredients:

- 2 cups tapioca pearl, cooked
- 1¼ cups banana, sliced
- 1/2 cup ripe jackfruit, sliced
- 4 cups coconut milk
- 1 cup white sugar
- 1½ cups sweet potato, diced
- 20 pcs rice balls
- 1 cup water
- 1/2 cup taro roots, diced

Instructions:

First, in a sauce pan, add the water and cook on high heat until it comes to boil.

Add about 1½ cups of coconut milk and cook for 5 minutes.

Add the sweet potatoes and taro roots and cook for 6 minutes.

Then, pour in the rest of the coconut milk.

Add the rice balls and sugar and cook for about 8 minutes.

Add the banana and cook for 2 minutes. Add the jackfruit and cook for another 2 minutes.

Finally, add the tapioca pearls and cook for 2 minutes. Serve warm.

Arroz Valenciana

This is not your ordinary risotto! It takes rice cooking to another level. Perfectly suited to celebrate Saints' day!

Preparation Time: 10 minutes

Cooking Time: 45 minutes

Serves: 6

Ingredients:

- 1 1/2 cups glutinous rice
- 1/2 cup oil
- ½ lb. shrimp
- ½ lb. pork liver
- 1 1/2 cups white rice
- 3 pcs chorizo, sliced
- 1 lb. pork loins
- ½ lb. chicken cubes
- 1 pinch saffron
- 1 onion, sliced
- 1 red bell pepper, sliced
- 1/4 tsp paprika
- 1 can green peas
- 3 eggs, hardboiled, sliced
- 3 pcs bay leaves
- Salt and pepper to taste

Instructions:

In a saucepan, add 6 cup of water. Add the pork loin, chicken cubes, bay leaves, onion and peppercorn. Cook for 10 minutes. Add the salt and shrimp and cook for 5 minutes.

Take the shrimp, chicken and pork out. Add the rice and cook for 20 minutes.

In a skillet, add the oil and fry the pork liver and chorizo with a pinch of salt and pepper.

Add the liver and chorizo into the rice mixture. Add the green peas and paprika and mix well. Cook for 3 minutes and serve hot with boiled eggs on top.

Cassava Cake

This cassava cake is easy to make and tastes very good. It is a perfect tribute to the saints.

Preparation Time: 15 minutes

Cooking Time: 1.5 hours

Serves: 8

Ingredients:

- 2 lb. grated cassava
- 3 egg whites
- 1 (14 oz) can condensed milk
- 3 eggs
- 1 (14 oz) can coconut milk
- 1 (13 oz) can coconut cream
- 1 (12 oz) can evaporated milk
- 1 cup grated coconut
- 2/3 cup sugar

Topping:

- 1/3 cup coconut milk
- 3 egg yokes
- 1/3 cup coconut cream
- 1/3 cup condensed milk

Instructions:

Preheat your oven to 350 degrees F.

Add all the cake ingredients in your mixing bowl.

Beat well and make a smooth mix.

Grease a square pan. Then, pour the mixture. Bake for about 1 hour.

In another bowl, combine the egg yolks, condense milk, coconut cream and coconut milk.

Mix well and add the topping. Bake for another 20 minutes. Serve cold.

Pichi Pichi

This cassava sweet treat is perfect for making your Saints' Day extra special. It just melts in your mouth! The coconut topping on top adds more flavor to it.

Preparation Time: 5 minutes

Cooking Time: 5 minutes

Serves: 2

Ingredients:

- 2 cups grated coconut
- 1½ cups water
- 1½ cups sugar
- 1 tsp pandan essence
- 1½ cups grated cassava

Instructions:

Squeeze out the juice from the grated cassava.

Combine the cassava, sugar, and water and mix well.

Add the pandan essence and sugar. Mix well.

Toast the bread slices and set aside for now.

Add the grated coconut and mix well.

Add the mix into your steamer.

Steam them for 30 minutes. Cut into slices and serve cold.

Coconut Jaggery Soul Cookies

These soul cookies are very unique with currants and jaggery. The preparation of making them is simple, and they taste very good to the soul.

Preparation Time: 30 minutes

Cooking Time: 15 minutes

Serves: 10 cookies

Ingredients:

- 2 1/4 cups flour
- 1/4 cup butter
- 1 tbsp cocoa powder
- 1 tsp orange zest
- 1/4 cup orange juice
- 1 egg
- 3 tbsp honey
- 1 cup jaggery
- 1 tsp cinnamon
- 1 tsp baking soda
- 1/2 cup raisins
- 1/2 cup chopped walnuts
- 1/4 tsp nutmeg
- 1 pinch sea salt
- Powdered sugar for garnish

Instructions:

Preheat the oven to 350 degrees F. Then, add parchment paper on your cookie sheet.

Beat the butter and jiggery in a mixing bowl.

Add the egg, honey, orange juice, and orange zest. Beat well.

Add the dry ingredients and fold into dough.

Wrap the dough and fridge for 20 minutes.

Roll the dough into 2 inch thickness and cut into 10 cookies.

Add the currants on top and press them to be firm into the surface.

Add to the cookies sheet and bake for 15 minutes. Serve after 20 minutes.

Lemon Chicken

The good thing about this chicken preparation is you do not have to spend too much time marinating it. You only need 15 minutes, and you are ready to grill it!

Preparation Time: 25 minutes

Cooking Time: 15 minutes

Serves: 4

Ingredients:

- 4 chicken breasts
- 1/4 cup Dijon mustard
- 2 tbsp lemon juice
- 1/2 tsp marjoram
- 1 tsp oil
- Salt to taste
- 2 tsp Worcestershire sauce
- Black pepper to taste

Instructions:

In a bowl, combine all the ingredients expect the chicken breasts.

Pound the chicken breasts with kitchen hammer.

Marinate the chicken in the mixture for 15 minutes.

Add some oil into the grilling pan. Grill the chicken for 6 minutes per side.

Serve after 5 minutes.

Nun Puffs

This recipe takes making nun to another level. On top of that, they look very adorable!

Preparation Time: 15 minutes

Cooking Time: 50 minutes

Serves: 9

Ingredients:

- ½ cup stick butter
- 1 cup milk
- ¾ cup flour
- 4 eggs
- 2 tbsp sesame seeds

Instructions:

Preheat the oven to 375 degrees F.

Use oil to grease your muffin pan.

In a pan, add the butter over medium heat.

Add the milk and cook for 10 minutes.

Add the flour and stir continuously.

Take off the heat. Then, let the mixture cool down.

Add the eggs and mix well. Use an ice cream scooper and add the mixture into the muffin pan.

Top with sesame seeds. Bake for 30 minutes. Serve at room temperature.

Polish Doughnuts – Pączki

These are not your average donuts! They are a posh and polish donut filled with jam of your choice. I have used fig jam here.

Preparation Time: 25 minutes

Cooking Time: 45 minutes

Serves: 12

Ingredients:

- 1 1/2 cups flour
- 2 egg yolks
- 1/4 cup sugar
- 2/3 cup warm milk
- 3 tbsp oil
- 1 tbsp melted butter
- 2 tsp yeast
- 1/4 tsp salt
- 1/2 tsp vanilla
- 1/3 cup sugar for coating
- 1 cup fig jam

Instructions:

In a bowl, combine the yeast with flour and salt.

Add the warm milk and mix well.

Let it sit for 10 minutes. Add the egg yolks, oil and vanilla. Mix well for 2 minutes. Knead for 5 minutes and let the dough rest for 10 minutes. Make 12 balls using your hands.

Add wax paper on your baking sheet. Add the little balls into the baking sheet.

Bake for about 45 minutes with 375 degrees F.

Let them cool down completely. Use a knife to make hole inside and fill the inside using the fig jam. Serve with granulated sugar on top.

Angel Food Cake

The name of the cake itself is perfect for celebrating Saints' day! This is a simple cake that will surely set the vibe for Saints' day.

Preparation Time: 15 minutes

Cooking Time: 35 minutes

Serves: 8

Ingredients:

- 12 egg whites
- 1 cup cake flour
- 1 1/2 tsp cream of tartar
- 2/3 cup sugar
- 1/4 tsp table salt
- 1/2 tsp almond extract
- 2/3 cup sugar
- 1 1/2 tsp vanilla extract

Instructions:

First, preheat oven to 375 degrees F.

In a bowl, shift the dry ingredients.

Next, beat the egg whites for 3 minutes in another bowl.

Add the salt and cream of tartar and beat well.

Then, add the dry ingredients gradually. Fold in using a spatula.

Add the batter in your cake pan. Tap the pan twice.

Bake for about 30 minutes. Serve in room temperature.

Sugar Cookie Bars

Saints' Day is not celebrated until you make some delicious desserts to honor the saints. This recipe is perfect for celebrating the holy day.

Preparation Time: 5 minutes

Cooking Time: 5 minutes

Serves: 2

Ingredients:

- 1/4 cup powdered sugar
- 3/4 cup butter
- 2 1/4 cups flour
- 1/2 tsp salt
- 2 eggs
- 1 tsp vanilla extract
- 3/4 cup granulated sugar
- 1/2 tbsp lemon zest
- 1 tsp baking powder

Frosting:

- 2 1/2 cups powdered sugar
- 6 tbsp butter, softened
- 1/4 tsp vanilla extract
- ¼ tsp pink food color
- 3 tbsp milk

Instructions:

Preheat oven to 375 degrees F.

Beat the frosting ingredients in a bowl. Keep it in the fridge until used.

Next, in a bowl, beat the sugars and butter for 5 minutes.

Add the eggs and beat for 2 minutes. Add the lemon zest and vanilla. Then, beat well.

Add the dry ingredients. Fold in gently.

Next, add wax paper onto a baking pan. Add the mixture and bake for 10 minutes.

Let it cool down completely. Add the frosting on top. Cut into squares and decorate further using sprinkles if you like.

Cinnamon spiced Soul cakes

These cakes are simple to make, and you can do variations like adding shredded coconut or currants in them. The texture is soft and delicious.

Preparation Time: 1.5 hours

Cooking Time: 15 minutes

Serves: 10

Ingredients:

- 1 cake yeast
- 1/2 cup butter
- 1/4 cup lukewarm water
- 2 cups scalded milk
- 1/2 cup sugar
- 6 cups flour
- ½ cup shredded coconut
- 2 tsp cinnamon
- 2 tsp salt
- 4 tbsp currants
- 1 egg, beaten

Instructions:

Preheat the oven to 350 degrees F. Then, add wax paper onto a cookie sheet.

Combine the lukewarm water with yeast.

Next, cover with a lid and let it sit for 10 minutes.

Beat the butter with sugar and milk and mix well.

Add the mixture into the yeast mixture.

Next, add the flour, shredded coconut and egg and mix well. Let it sit for 1 hour with a lid on top.

Knead well and roll it into 2 inch thickness. Cut into rounds. Add to the cookie sheet.

Add the currants on top. Bake for about 15 minutes and let it cool down. Serve.

DOUGHNUTS

These are not your average donuts. The whole wheat, cinnamon and nutmeg add a different flavor and texture to them.

Preparation Time: 30 minutes

Cooking Time: 10 minutes

Serves: 10

Ingredients:

- 4 cups whole wheat flour
- 4 tsp baking powder
- 2 beaten eggs
- 1 cup milk
- 5 tbsp melted shortening
- 1/2 tsp salt
- 1/2 tsp nutmeg
- 1 cup sugar
- 1/2 tsp cinnamon

Instructions:

Combine the milk, sugar, egg and shortening.

Beat well. Shift the dry ingredients twice.

Add the dry ingredients into the milk mixture.

Make dough and let it sit for 30 minutes. Roll it out and use a donut cutter to cut into 10 donuts.

Fry the donuts in batches in the deep fryer.

Roll them in granulated sugar and cinnamon powder before serving. This step is optional.

Frosty Pumpkin Dessert

This is a special pie made with love! The crust itself is very soft and perfectly melts in your mouth. The topping is done in two layers which adds more flavor to it.

Preparation Time: 10 hours

Cooking Time: no cooking required

Serves: 16

Ingredients:

- 1 1/3 cups gingersnap cookies, crumbled
- 2/3 cup toffee bits
- 1/4 cup butter, melted
- 2 1/2 cups whipped topping, divided
- 2 tsp cinnamon spice blend
- 1 cup pumpkin puree, cooked
- 1 container vanilla ice cream (1/2 gallon), divided
- 1/3 cup brown sugar

Instructions:

Grease a spring form pan and add wax paper on the bottom.

Combine the crumbled cookies with butter. Mix well.

Add to the pan and let it fridge for 2 hours.

Take half of the ice cream in a bowl. Add 1 cup of whipped topping and the toffee bits.

Blend for 1 minute. Add onto the crust. Freeze for 1 hour.

Combine the remaining ice cream with pumpkin puree.

Add the remaining whipped topping, sugar and spice mix.

Beat well and add to the pie. Freeze for another 8 hours. Serve.

Tinga

This dish is so quick and simple that you would be surprised how delicious it turns out afterwards. Fill it into your tortillas or tacos and enjoy!

Preparation Time: 5 minutes

Cooking Time: 20 minutes

Serves: 4

Ingredients:

- 1 lb. hamburger meat
- 1 1/2 cups water
- 2 onions, chopped
- 1 tsp cumin
- 1 tsp garlic powder
- 1 tbsp cornstarch
- 1/2 tsp black pepper
- Salt to taste

Instructions:

In a skillet, add the meat and stir until they become brown.

Add the onion and cook for 3 minutes.

Add the water mixed with cornstarch and stir continuously for 5 minutes.

Add the salt, pepper, garlic and cumin. Cook for 5 minutes. Serve hot.

Hot Cross Buns

Hot cross buns are everyone's favorite. You cannot imagine celebrating a special event without having them on the table.

Preparation Time: 2 hours

Cooking Time: 20 minutes

Serves: 20

Ingredients:

- 1/2 cup sugar
- 2 cups whole milk
- 1 pkg active dry yeast
- 4 cups all-purpose flour
- 1/2 cup raisins
- 1/2 cup flour
- 1/2 cup canola oil
- 1/2 tsp baking powder
- 1/2 tsp baking soda
- 1/4 cup sugar
- 1 tsp cinnamon
- 2 tsp salt

Instructions:

First, combine the sugar with milk and oil in a large mixing bowl. Mix well and heat until it becomes warm.

Add the yeast and stir well. Then, cover and let it sit for 10 minutes.

Add the all-purpose flour and make dough. Cover again. Let it sit for 1 hour.

Next, add the remaining flour, salt, baking powder, and baking soda. Add some sugar and cinnamon and mix well. Knead for 5 minutes. Divide into 20 buns and add a wax paper on your baking sheet.

Then, place the buns and let them rise for 10 minutes. Brush the top using egg wash. Bake for 20 minutes. Let them cool down. Add any icing of your choice. Serve.

Beef Stew

If you are looking for a wholesome savory main dish for Saints' day, this beef dish will do the trick!

Preparation Time: 15 minutes

Cooking Time: 1.5 hours

Serves: 8

Ingredients:

- 1 1/4 lb. beef, cut into chunks
- 2 cups water
- Salt and pepper to taste
- 1 cup white vinegar
- 1/4 cup olive oil
- 4 cups beef stock
- 1 large onion, chopped
- 3 lb. potatoes, peeled, diced
- 6 garlic cloves, minced
- 1 tbsp dried thyme
- 1 cup Guinness extra stout
- 1 tbsp sugar
- 1 tbsp Worcestershire sauce
- 2 tbsp tomato paste
- 2 bay leaves
- 2 tbsp butter
- 2 cups carrots, diced
- 2 tbsp chopped parsley

Instructions:

Coat the beef into salt and pepper and fry them for 5 minutes with oil in a saucepan.

Next, add the garlic and onion. Sauté for 2 minutes.

Pour in the water and the stock. Cook for 5 minutes.

Add the vinegar, sugar, thyme, tomato paste, Worcestershire sauce, Guinness and bay leaves.

Next, cover and cook for 20 minutes. Simmer for another 40 minutes.

In another pan, add some oil. Fry the potatoes and carrots with a pinch of salt and pepper until they are golden.

Add the vegetables into the stew. Cook for 30 minutes. Serve hot with parsley.

Grasshopper Pie

This pie is special, and it looks like a giant chocolate cookie. It will be a favorite for both kids and adults during the Saints' day celebration.

Preparation Time: 5 hours

Cooking Time: 10 minutes

Serves: 8

Ingredients:

- 1 cup heavy cream
- Extra cookie crumbs, to garnish
- 2 tbsp creme de cacao liqueur
- 24 marshmallows
- 2 tbsp butter, melted
- 2 tbsp creme de menthe liqueur
- 2/3 cup half-and-half
- 16 chocolate sandwich cookies

Instructions:

Grease a pie pan. In a food processor, add the cookies and butter.

Blend until it becomes crumbly. Add to the pie pan. Evenly spread.

In a pan, combine the marshmallows with the half-and-half. Keep the heat to low.

Stir continuously for 3 minutes. Take off the heat. Then, let it cool down.

Add the creme de cacao and creme de menthe to the mixture. Mix well.

In another bowl, beat the heavy cream for 5 minutes. Add the marshmallow mix into the heavy cream mix and fold in using a spatula. Add to the crust. Freeze for 4 hours. Serve.

St. Martin's Mini Mice Cupcakes

What better way to celebrate Saints' day then having mini mice cupcakes that are too adorable to resist.

Preparation Time: 30 minutes

Cooking Time: 12 minutes

Serves: 12 cupcakes

Ingredients:

- 1 pkg chocolate cake mix
- 1 cup white frosting
- 1 container chocolate frosting
- Candy wafers to decorate
- m&m's to decorate
- Black string licorice

Instructions:

First, preheat oven to 350 degrees F. Add muffin liners onto your muffin tray.

In a mixing bowl, prepare the chocolate cake mix following the direction written in the box.

Next, pour the batter into the muffin liners.

Bake in the oven for 12 minutes. Let them cool down completely.

Add the white frosting and chocolate frosting. Decorate using the items to resemble mice.

Hungarian Cinnamon Bread

The Hungarian bread is perfect to set the mood for celebrating Saints' day. You can custom make the filling according to your choice.

Preparation Time: 2 hours

Cooking Time: 30 minutes

Serves: 10

Ingredients:

- 4 cups all-purpose flour
- 1/4 cup melted butter
- 1/4 cup white sugar
- 1 egg
- 1 tsp cinnamon
- 1¼ cups warm milk
- 1 pkg active dry yeast
- 1 tsp salt
- 1 tsp vanilla extract
- 1/3 cup brown sugar

Instructions:

Shift the dry ingredients in a bowl.

Next, in another bowl, beat the egg with the sugar. Add the butter and vanilla and beat well.

Combine the yeast with warm milk. Let it sit for 10 minutes.

Add the butter mix and flour mix. Fold into dough. Knead well and cover with lid for 1 hour.

Knead again and roll out on a surface.

Next, combine the brown sugar with cinnamon and add on top of the rolled dough. Roll the dough and place on your greased baking sheet.

Then, bake for 30 minutes with 350 degrees F.

Cut into slices and serve in room temperature.

Rolled Spiced Rye Sticks

These cinnamon and clove spiced breadsticks are of soft texture. They are a hit among both kids and adults. They go well with any dips or by itself.

Preparation Time: 20 minutes

Cooking Time: 20 minutes

Serves: 10

Ingredients:

- 2 cups rye flour
- 1 tsp baking powder
- 2/3 cup brown sugar
- ½ cup warm milk
- 1 tbsp honey
- 1 tsp cinnamon
- ½ tsp clove
- 1 pinch sea salt
- ½ cup butter
- 1 egg

Instructions:

Preheat the oven to 390 degrees F.

Grease a baking sheet using cooking spray.

Shift the flour, salt, cinnamon, clove and baking powder.

In a bowl, combine the egg and brown sugar and beat well.

Add the butter, honey and milk. Beat well.

Mix the dry ingredients and make dough.

Knead well for 6 minutes. Add to the baking sheet.

Bake for 20 minutes. Let it cool down. Cut into 4 inch lengthwise long sticks.

Sprinkle some granulated sugar on top before serving.

Apricot Currants Soul Cookies

These cookies are slightly different and soft in texture. You can decorate them as you wish. I have used currants and dried apricots on top. A pinch of saffron also adds more flavor and color to them.

Preparation Time: 20 minutes

Cooking Time: 15 minutes

Serves: 12 cookies

Ingredients:

- 2 cups all-purpose flour
- ½ cup cream cheese
- ½ cup apricot puree
- ½ cup sugar
- 1 tsp baking powder
- 1 pinch baking soda
- 1 pinch salt
- 4 tbsp currants
- 4 tbsp dried apricots, chopped
- 1 egg
- ¼ tsp saffron+1 tbsp warm milk
- ½ cup butter

Instructions:

Beat the egg in a bowl. Add the sugar and beat well.

Add the butter, cream cheese, saffron milk, and apricot puree. Beat well.

Add the dry ingredients and fold into dough. Refrigerate them for 10 minutes.

Preheat the oven to 400 degrees F. Add parchment paper on your cookie sheet.

Roll out the dough and cut rounds. Add them on the cookie sheet.

Add the apricots and currants on top. Bake for 15 minutes. Serve in room temperature.

Pecan Sweet Potato Balls

These balls are soft and gooey from the inside and crunchy and very flavorful from the outside.

Preparation Time: 35 minutes

Cooking Time: 10 minutes

Serves: 4 lb.

Ingredients:

- 4 cups almond meal, toasted
- 2½ cups sugar
- 1 pinch sea salt
- 1 cup boiled sweet potato
- 1 pinch cinnamon
- ½ tsp lemon zest
- 2 cups pine nuts
- 4 tbsp honey

Instructions:

First, in a mixing bowl, mash the sweet potatoes.

Add the sea salt, cinnamon, lemon zest, and sugar. Mix well.

Next, add the almond meal and mix again. Use your hands and make round balls.

In a pan, combine the pine nuts with honey and toss for 5 minutes.

Roll the balls in the pine nuts mixture. Let it set for 30 minutes. Serve.

Shrimp Cheese Noodle Salad

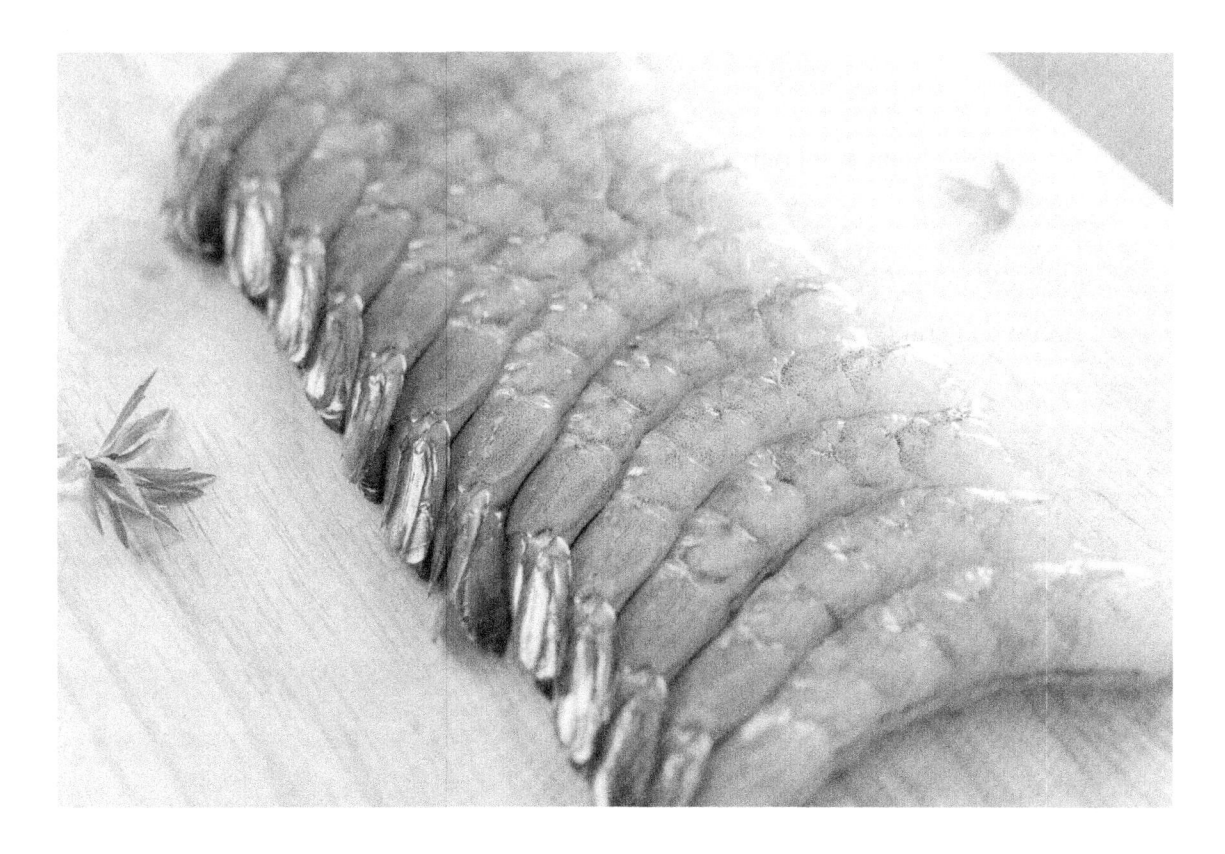

This noodle salad is amazing and perfect to celebrate Saints' day.

Preparation Time: 20 minutes

Cooking Time: 20 minutes

Serves: 4

Ingredients:

- 1 cup medium sized shrimp, with skin
- 1 red onion, chopped
- 1 cup lettuce leaves, chopped
- 2 cups noodles
- Salt and pepper to taste
- 1 cup baby radish, halved
- 4 eggs
- 1 tsp butter
- 10 green olives, pitted
- ½ cup mozzarella cubes
- 1 tsp tamarind pulp
- 2 tbsp lime juice
- 2 tbsp honey
- 1 tsp rosemary, minced
- ½ tsp oregano

Instructions:

In a pot, hard boil the eggs.

In another pot, boil the noodles in salted water. Drain and let it cool down.

In a skillet, add the butter and toss the shrimp with salt and pepper for 3 minutes.

Remove the shell of the eggs. Cut into wedges.

Combine the lettuce, radish, onion, noodles, shrimp and olives in a salad bowl.

Add the mozzarella cubes, eggs and mix.

Combine the lime juice, honey, salt, pepper, rosemary, oregano and tamarind pulp.

Mix well and add to the salad. Serve.

Mashed Potatoes

Mashed potatoes are a very basic item for any get-togethers, but you cannot really do without it either. So, for special days like Saints' Day, you need to try a unique mashed potato recipe like this one.

Preparation Time: 10 minutes

Cooking Time: 20 minutes

Serves: 4

Ingredients:

- 4 large potatoes, peeled
- ½ cup ripe avocado puree
- ½ cup spring onion, chopped
- ¼ tsp garlic powder
- Salt and pepper to taste
- 1 tsp parsley, chopped
- 2 tsp butter
- ¼ tsp cayenne pepper

Instructions:

Hard boil the potatoes with a pinch of salt.

Mash it finely. Add the salt, pepper, cayenne, half of butter, and garlic powder.

Mix well and add the avocado puree, spring onion and parsley. Mix again.

Serve with butter cube on top.

Blueberry Pancakes

These are a special blueberry pancake that is perfect to start your celebration of Saints' Day. Certainly, you can use any fruit of your choice for this recipe.

Preparation Time: 15 minutes

Cooking Time: 15 minutes

Serves: 4

Ingredients:

- 1 cup coconut flour
- ½ cup all-purpose flour
- 1 tsp baking powder
- 2 eggs
- ½ cup fresh blueberries
- 1 pinch salt
- ½ cup sugar
- 4 tsp olive oil
- 1 drop vanilla extract

Instructions:

First, in a large mixing bowl, beat the eggs.

Add the sugar and beat well. Add the olive oil, vanilla and mix.

Next, add the salt, baking powder and flours and fold into a smooth mix.

Add the blueberries and fold in. Let it sit for 10 minutes.

In a muffin mould, pour in the batter. Bake for 15 minutes with 380 degrees F.

Serve.

Chia Seed Spelt Bread

This is special bread because it takes real effort and time to make it, Chia Seed Artisan Bread from scratch.

Preparation Time: 5 hours

Cooking Time: 20 minutes

Serves: 8

Ingredients:

- 2 cups spelt flour
- 1 tsp baking powder
- 2 tsp dry active yeast
- ½ cup butter
- ½ cup warm milk
- ½ tsp salt
- 2 tbsp honey
- 4 tbsp chia seeds

Instructions:

First, shift the spelt flour, baking powder, and salt together.

In a bowl, combine the honey, warm milk and yeast. Mix well.

Next, cover and let it sit for 10 minutes.

Add the flour mix and mix well. Add the butter and mix again.

Knead for 10 minutes. Cover with a wet towel. Let it sit for 2 hours.

Then, knead again for 10 minutes. Again cover and let it sit for 2 hours.

Knead again and add to a baking sheet. Sprinkle the chia seeds on top.

Bake for 25 minutes with 360 degrees F.

Serve.

Conclusion

Saints' Day is a day to celebrate the spirit of positivity and what you believe in. Undoubtedly, food is one of the most common things that can bring people closer to each other and spread positivity. This e-book is filled with 30 recipes that are perfect to set the vibe of Saints' Day. Try the recipes yourself and celebrate the positivity that Saints' Day has to offer.

About the Author

Born in New Germantown, Pennsylvania, Stephanie Sharp received a Masters degree from Penn State in English Literature. Driven by her passion to create culinary masterpieces, she applied and was accepted to The International Culinary School of the Art Institute where she excelled in French cuisine. She has married her cooking skills with an aptitude for business by opening her own small cooking school where she teaches students of all ages.

Stephanie's talents extend to being an author as well and she has written over 400 e-books on the art of cooking and baking that include her most popular recipes.

Sharp has been fortunate enough to raise a family near her hometown in Pennsylvania where she, her husband and children live in a beautiful rustic house on an extensive piece of land. Her other passion is taking care of the furry members of her family which include 3 cats, 2 dogs and a potbelly pig named Wilbur.

Watch for more amazing books by Stephanie Sharp coming out in the next few months.

Author's Afterthoughts

I am truly grateful to you for taking the time to read my book. I cherish all of my readers! Thanks ever so much to each of my cherished readers for investing the time to read this book!

With so many options available to you, your choice to buy my book is an honour, so my heartfelt thanks at reading it from beginning to end!

I value your feedback, so please take a moment to submit an honest and open review on Amazon so I can get valuable insight into my readers' opinions and others can benefit from your experience.

Thank you for taking the time to review!

Stephanie Sharp

For announcements about new releases, please follow my author page on Amazon.com!

You can find that at:

https://www.amazon.com/author/stephanie-sharp

*or Scan **QR-code** below.*

Printed in Great Britain
by Amazon